My senses
help me

Bobbie Kalman

Crabtree Publishing Company

www.crabtreebooks.com

Created by Bobbie Kalman

Author and Editor-in-Chief
Bobbie Kalman

Educational consultants
Joan King
Reagan Miller
Elaine Hurst

Editors
Reagan Miller
Joan King
Kathy Middleton

Proofreader
Crystal Sikkens

Design
Bobbie Kalman
Katherine Berti

Photo research
Bobbie Kalman

Production coordinator
Katherine Berti

Prepress technician
Katherine Berti

Photographs
iStockphoto: p. 4 (bottom)
Shutterstock: cover, p. 1, 3, 4 (top), 5, 6, 7, 8, 9, 10,
    11, 12, 13, 14 (bottom left), 15 (except top right)
Other photographs by Comstock and Photodisc

Library and Archives Canada Cataloguing in Publication

Kalman, Bobbie, 1947-
    My senses help me / Bobbie Kalman.

(My world)
ISBN 978-0-7787-9428-8 (bound).--ISBN 978-0-7787-9472-1 (pbk.)

    1. Senses and sensation--Juvenile literature. I. Title.
II. Series: My world (St. Catharines, Ont.)

QP434.K355 2010   j612.8   C2009-906064-7

Library of Congress Cataloging-in-Publication Data

Kalman, Bobbie.
 My senses help me / Bobbie Kalman.
    p. cm. -- (My world)
 ISBN 978-0-7787-9472-1 (pbk. : alk. paper) -- ISBN 978-0-7787-9428-8
(reinforced library binding : alk. paper)
 1. Senses and sensation--Juvenile literature. I. Title.

 QP434.K355 2010
 612.8--dc22

                                        2009041180

Crabtree Publishing Company

Printed in China/122009/CT20091009

www.crabtreebooks.com   1-800-387-7650

Published in Canada
Crabtree Publishing
616 Welland Ave.
St. Catharines, Ontario
L2M 5V6

Published in the United States
Crabtree Publishing
PMB 59051
350 Fifth Avenue, 59th Floor
New York, New York 10118

Published in the United Kingdom
Crabtree Publishing
Maritime House
Basin Road North, Hove
BN41 1WR

Published in Australia
Crabtree Publishing
386 Mt. Alexander Rd.
Ascot Vale (Melbourne)
VIC 3032

Words to know

glasses

listening

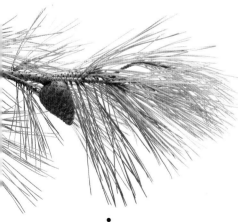
pine
needles

skunk

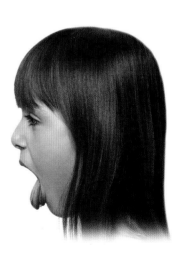
tongue

3

I have
five senses.

I can hear.

I can see.

I can taste.   I can smell.

I can touch.

I see with my eyes.
I am looking at a girl.
Do you see her **glasses**?
Her glasses help her see better.

My eyes can see colors.

I am painting with a lot of colors.

Which colors do you see?

I hear with my ears.
My friend is talking to me.
I am **listening** to him.

8

My mother is reading us a story.
We are all listening
because it is a great story!

I smell with my nose.
I smell a **skunk**.
"Yuck! That stinks."

I taste with my **tongue**.
This strawberry tastes great!

I touch with my fingers.
I am touching **pine needles**.
"Ouch! They are very sharp."

I feel with my skin.
"That water feels really cold. Brrrr!"

Activity

Which food tastes sweet?

Which food tastes sour?

Which food tastes salty?

Which food tastes spicy?

peppers

lemon

banana

popcorn

pizza

watermelon

15

Notes for adults

Enjoyment or warning?

Our senses help us enjoy our world. We love to smell flowers, taste delicious foods, listen to music, look at beautiful scenery, and touch and feel soft things. Our senses also warn us of danger. Hearing a dog barking, seeing cars coming when we cross the road, smelling smoke, tasting something that has gone bad, and feeling hot surfaces all warn us of dangers. With the help of your class, make one chart of things that our senses enjoy and another showing possible dangers about which our senses warn us.

Touch-and-feel box

Create a touch-and-feel box. Choose objects of various textures and place them in a box. Cover the box with a cloth. Ask the children to reach under the cloth and identify the objects by the way they feel—smooth, rough, sharp, bumpy, soft. After they have identified all the objects, ask them to group them according to their textures.

What other meanings does the word "feel" have? Ask the children to use the word in different ways.

How does it feel? looks at various textures in nature and the words used to describe how they feel, such as rough, soft, silky, smooth, or bumpy.
Guided Reading: I

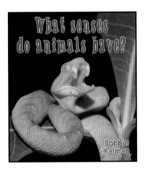

What senses do animals have? is a fascinating book about the usual, as well as, super senses of animals.
Guided Reading: M